How do I use this scheme?

Key Words with Peter and Jane has three
parallel series, each containing twelve books. All three
series are written using the same carefully controlled
vocabulary. Readers will get the most out of **Key Words** with
Peter and Jane when they follow the books in the pattern
1a, 1b, 1c; 2a, 2b, 2c and so on.

• Series a
gradually introduces and repeats new words.

• Series b
provides further practice of these same words, but
in a different context and with different illustrations.

• Series c
uses familiar words to teach **phonics** in a methodical way,
enabling children to read increasingly difficult words.
It also provides a link to writing.

LADYBIRD BOOKS

UK | USA | Canada | Ireland | Australia
India | New Zealand | South Africa

Ladybird Books is part of the Penguin Random House group of companies
whose addresses can be found at global.penguinrandomhouse.com.

www.penguin.co.uk   www.puffin.co.uk   www.ladybird.co.uk

First published 1964
This edition 2009, 2014, 2016
Copyright © Ladybird Books Ltd, 1964
001

Key Words

with Peter and Jane

11c Books are exciting

written by W. Murray
illustrated by M. Aitchison and J.H. Wingfield

This boy and girl are beginning to read well. Their names are Tim and Rita. To make reading more interesting and to help them to learn more quickly at school, they each have a free choice book as well as a book in their reading scheme. They can take this free choice book from the book corner, where attractive books are set out on show. There are many different kinds of books to be seen. Nearly all of them have attractive pictures.

"It makes me want to read more and more when I see so many interesting books," says Rita to her friend.

"Yes," answers Tim, "I like reading. Some of the books are very exciting. I like adventure stories best."

"I like adventure stories, too," says the girl, "but school stories and books about animals are good." She looks through a book made by another girl. It is a large scrapbook about her pets.

Tim finds a book about football, and then another about cowboys and Indians. After this he picks up a book about astronauts and spaceships. Then at last he decides which book to read – it is a story of adventure under the sea.

In the book Tim chooses from the book corner there is a story about treasure found on the sea-bed. Many years ago, near a lonely island, a pirate ship ran into some rocks during a storm. The pirate ship sank and the treasure on board went down with it. The pirates were all drowned.

Years later, a boy and his sister were near this island in their father's boat. They had stopped near the place where the pirate ship sank. The brother and sister dived into the water to explore the sea-bed and found a metal box near some rocks. It was part of the treasure from the pirate ship.

As they tried to move the box they saw an octopus in the rocks near them. They were afraid that this octopus might attack them, so they left the metal box by the rocks and went back to their boat.

Then their father and another man dived with them to get the treasure. Each of the men had a knife to use if the octopus should attack them. However, it did not do so, and they brought the box of treasure up to their boat.

'My holiday' is the title of the book Rita takes from the book corner. This book has been made by her friend named Rose. In it, Rose has stuck souvenirs of her holiday. She has written about these souvenirs on the pages.

One of the souvenirs is a photograph of Rose on a pony in the heather at the top of a hill. Some of the heather from the hillside is stuck on the same page. There is also a large picture of a hovercraft in which Rita and her brother had a ride. It was the first time they had been in a hovercraft.

There are some postcards in the book. One shows some people in fancy dress in a carnival procession. Some have large masks on their faces, and others hold balloons or throw streamers. Everyone is happy in the picture on the postcard.

Rita looks on through the book. She reads how Rose learned to swim and to row a boat. There is a picture of a lighthouse that Rose and her brother went over.

Rita finds the book very interesting and decides to make a book about her own holiday next year.

y Pony

This Heather
was here

My first row.

T
ro
Ne
he

Carnival.

HOVERCRAFT

We went on this

Tim is now reading about a cowboy who had caught some wild horses. The cowboy wanted to tame the horses, so that men could ride them. Then he could sell the horses for a lot of money.

However, taming a wild horse is not easy. No wild horse likes a man to be near it. It does not like a saddle on its back or a rope round its head. Least of all does it like a man on its back.

In the old days a heavy saddle was put on the wild horse at once. Then the cowboy climbed into the saddle and tried to stay there as the horse ran, jumped and kicked. It was very hard to stay in the saddle. Sometimes the horse threw the man off its back onto the ground. Sometimes it kicked the man very hard.

Nowadays much more care is taken in taming a wild horse. The cowboy lets the horse get to know him before he rides it. It takes longer to tame a horse this way but it is kinder and safer.

It may take days or even weeks before a wild horse is tamed enough for a man to ride it quietly.

The title of the book Rita has now chosen from the book corner is 'Tricks and Games.' It is a book with descriptions of interesting and useful things that young children can make or do. Each page has printed instructions and attractive pictures for the reader.

Rita reads about invisible writing. This means writing that you cannot see. If you write on paper with the juice of an onion (or lemon), the writing is invisible at first. However, if you heat the paper, the writing appears and can then be read quite easily.

The girl decides to send a secret message to a friend, for fun. It will be in invisible writing. She gets some lemon juice and a pen and some paper. Then she writes with the juice. After the juice has dried she puts the paper in an envelope and sends it to a friend.

The next day Rita calls on her friend, who tells her that she has had a blank piece of paper through the post. She is surprised when she learns that it is a secret letter. Then the two girls heat the piece of paper and the writing appears. The secret letter can then be read.

Dear Peggy,
I am writing
this letter with
lemon juice
instead of
ink.
Rita.

In the book corner there are some interesting books about the human body. These have many illustrations and descriptions of different parts of the human body. The illustrations show the inside of the body as well as the outside, and the descriptions are set out clearly so that children can understand them.

When boys and girls understand what the human body is and how it works, they look after it more carefully and so keep healthy.

The body needs sunshine, fresh air and exercise. It also needs different kinds of food and drink. Boys and girls will not grow into healthy men and women if they do not have enough food and drink of the right kind. The book explains which kinds are needed. Some people may be too fat or too thin because they eat too much or too little.

We must also have work and rest to keep healthy. Some children do not get enough sleep because they go to bed too late.

We must brush our teeth so that they will not go bad. We wash so that we keep clean and healthy and fresh.

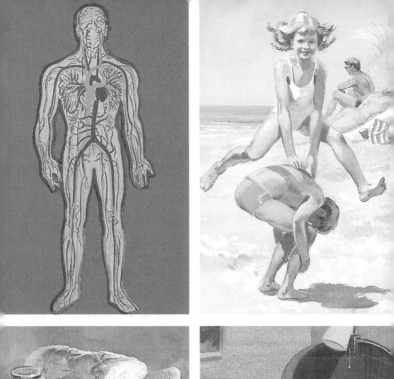

Peter and Jane are making a collection of books of their own which they keep at home. They have been given a bookcase for these books. The shelves are not high and can be reached easily by both of them. They have half the shelves each but borrow books freely from each other.

The two children get some books as presents from friends and relations. Most of these books are given to them on their birthdays or at Christmas. They buy other books with their own money.

Some of the books in their own collection have been made by Peter and Jane themselves. Most of these home-made books are collections of photographs, stamps, postcards, cut-out pictures, or leaves and flowers. There is a Safety First book which Peter made and a book of drawings by Jane. They are making a television book together. This has pictures and news of the people they like to watch on television.

If you looked through Peter and Jane's shelves in the bookcase you would see books about adventure, aeroplanes and spaceships, treasure hunts, animals and sports. They also have books about fairy stories, nature and school stories.

Sometimes the brother and sister exchange books with relations and friends.

Jane and some friends are going to have a picnic in the woods. It has been dry, hot weather for a long time and they will be careful as there may be poisonous snakes about.

Jane goes to her bookcase to see what the books can tell her about the adder. She finds a nature book with the title, *What to look for in Summer,* and turns to the index at the back. In this index she sees 'Adder . . . Page 40,' and soon she is looking at the coloured picture of an adder and reading about it.

She learns that it is the only poisonous snake found in England, and that it usually keeps away from people. Adders are just as much afraid of people as people are of adders.

Jane takes the book with her to show her friends and then they all go off to the woods. As they walk by the trees and bushes they keep a sharp look-out for snakes.

They come to a place where some trees have been cut down. Suddenly they clearly see an adder on a tree stump in the sunshine. They stand still and the adder slides away.

Peter and Jane's friends like to borrow the book about skin-divers and exploring under the sea. The book explains what skin-divers use when they are under the water.

A face mask helps the skin-diver to see clearly. Breathing tubes give him air to breathe while he is under the water. This air comes from two metal tubes which are on the diver's back.

To move along he can swim or use an under-water scooter. This scooter has a motor which makes it move quite quickly on or under the water. The diver holds on to the underwater scooter by two handles, and is pulled along without having to move his arms or legs.

The skin-diver should wear a life-jacket as there are many dangers under the sea. This life-jacket is coloured red and can be blown up quickly from a tube of air. Many skin-divers would have been drowned but for a life-jacket of this kind.

Some divers hunt big fish for sport. Children always like to read about the underwater speargun which skin-divers can use for this. The speargun shoots a spear which can kill a large fish.

This picture is from another exciting adventure book from the children's bookcase. It is about a rescue by helicopter.

Two boys went to a ruined castle by the sea to look for birds. They knew that birds' nests were to be seen in the ivy on the walls of the ruined castle.

One boy used an old stone staircase to get to the top of a high wall. Just as he climbed from the staircase on to the wall, the staircase collapsed and crashed to the ground. The boy then found that he could not get down from the high wall. He tried to climb down the ivy but it was not strong enough. His friend could not climb up far enough to help.

After a while the boy on the ground went to get help from a farm that was near. The farmer telephoned the airfield for a helicopter to take the boy off the wall. He knew that a fire engine could not be driven close enough to the ruined castle to help.

Before long a helicopter arrived over the castle. A man from it was let down on a rope to the boy, and then both the boy and the man were pulled up into the helicopter.

One of the nature books in the children's collection is about life under water. There is a description of the octopus which lives among rocks in warm seas. At some seaside places the octopus is called a devil fish, as many people are afraid of it.

The octopus, or devil fish, has eight long arms and a body which is generally yellow. Its two eyes are large and staring.

Most octopuses are quite small. However, there are some bigger ones, and a few that are very large. They do not generally attack humans.

Octopuses swim by squirting out water and are able to move along quickly in this way. If they are attacked they can squirt a kind of dark ink into the water.

The book has a story of how some islanders in the South Seas catch octopuses for food. These are quite small ones, so there is not much danger from them.

Two South Sea islanders work together to catch the octopus. One man dives into the water near an octopus so that it can put some of its arms round his body or legs. Then the other man pulls his friend and the octopus out of the water.

Peter has a book about a country on the other side of the world. This country is Australia. He has been learning about it at school and now he wants to find out more about this interesting land.

There are forests of giant trees in Australia. One kind of these giant trees is called the Karri tree and this can be much taller than the tall churches in Peter's own country. The Karri tree is one of the tallest trees in the world, and its wood is very strong.

The picture which Peter is looking at, is of a very tall Karri tree with a little cabin made of wood right at the top. Peter is thinking of their own little house in a tree which their father made for them. However, the cabin in the Karri tree is not a playhouse. It has been put there as a look-out post.

Peter shows the picture to Jane. They talk about it and then read the page opposite. It tells them why the look-out post is in the Karri tree. As the cabin is so high, a forest fire can be seen from it while the fire is still a long way away.

In one of the books, Jane has been reading how sweets are made. Now she finds out something about chocolate. She learns that chocolate is made from cocoa beans. Cocoa pods, with these beans inside, grow on cocoa trees. Cocoa trees grow in Ghana, in Africa.

Jane gets a map of Africa to see where Ghana is. She learns that it is a hot country.

The cocoa pods are cut from the trees, and the beans taken from the pods and put in the sun to dry. Then the beans are put in sacks and sent to this country. Here they are taken from the sacks and roasted. After the beans have been roasted, they are put into machines which grind them into rich, liquid chocolate.

Milk is then added to this liquid, and more machines make the milk and chocolate into a smooth mixture. The chocolates we know so well are then made from this mixture, and taken to shops all over the country.

Jane then reads about other trees and the things that are made from them.

Jane and Peter do not go to school on Saturday. Every week on this day they go to the shops in their home town. One of the shops at which they like to call is a large book shop. Here there are not only books but comics and papers on sale.

They look at the comics first and buy one each. Now that they can read well they not only look at the pictures but also read the stories. When they have read their own comics they often exchange them with other children.

There are many colourful and attractive books on show. Peter and Jane enjoy looking at these. Sometimes they choose a book for themselves. A relation has just given each of them a book token, so today they wish to exchange the tokens for two books to add to their own collections. They find that it is hard to choose as there are so many good books on sale.

They look through many books and choose one about pets. This tells them how to keep their own pets healthy and happy.

They look through a book about swimming. Then they look through the books and choose one about motor cars. They want to know more about car engines.

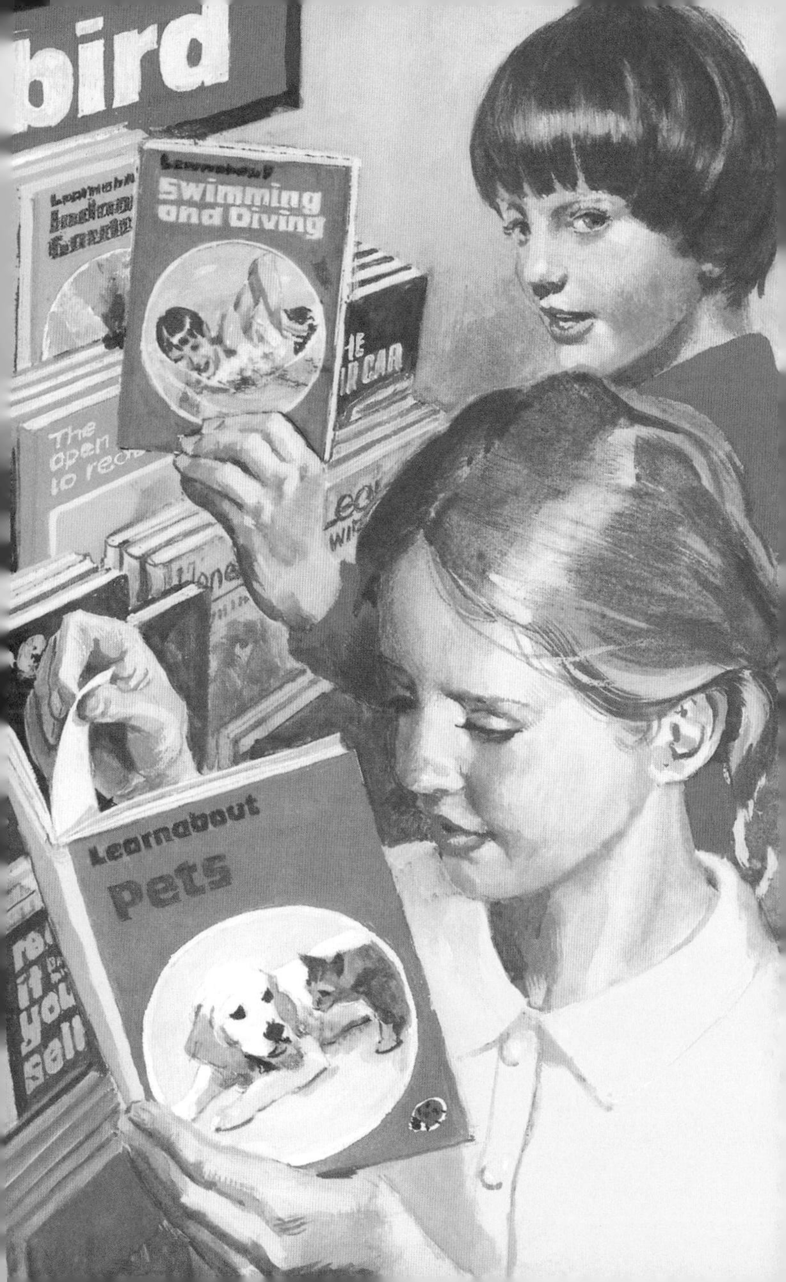
bird
Swimming and Diving
Learnabout
Pets

Every year, about Christmas time, Peter has an Annual given to him. This is one of many large books which come out annually, which means once a year. It has a collection of stories and as well as these, there are pictures, puzzles, crosswords, games, jokes, and other items of interest to young readers.

Jane is given an Annual at the same time as Peter. Hers is the same size and Jane's Annual also has stories, pictures, puzzles, crosswords, games and jokes.

The Annuals are not only interesting to read, but they give the children ideas for things to do when they have to stay in the house on wet days.

One of the games in Peter's book is called 'The Donkey's Tail.' They often play it when other children come to tea. Someone draws a large picture of a donkey without a tail. Then, one by one, with eyes covered, each boy and girl tries to pin the tail on the donkey. Everyone laughs a lot during this game.

The father of Peter and Jane told the two children that they should join the town library. He said that the library was like a gateway to interesting and exciting places. Although it looked just another building, a visit to it could take them, in imagination, to see the wonders of the world. Once they were through the gateway they could learn anything they wished through the books they chose. From books they could get not only information and knowledge, but interest and excitement.

The children went to the Junior Department of the library. They were given a card to fill in, so that they could join. Then their father had to sign the card to show that he agreed to pay for any lost or damaged books.

After this the children were each given library tickets. With these they could each take out two books from the Junior Department of the library.

There were more books at the library than the two children had ever seen before. The young lady in charge was very kind and explained what they had to do. She helped them to find some interesting books. Then she took their tickets and stamped the books with the date before the children took them away.

Peter's first book from the library was about that part of the earth which is under the sea. He read that there is more of the surface of the earth under the water than there is above it, but that little of this underwater world has so far been explored. Man has not learned how to live under the water for very long at a time.

Every year, man is learning more about the surface of the earth under the sea. He is also finding out how to stay under the water for a longer time. It is thought that one day there will be cities under the sea, just as there are cities on those parts of the earth which are above water. Men in these underwater cities will be able to dig deep below the surface of the earth to find oil, coal and other treasures that are valued so much. Gas and oil are now taken for our use from the rocks under the sea-bed.

The sea itself will give man much of value. Many kinds of valuable salts can be taken from sea water. Fish farms could be made which would give man many more fish than he can catch now.

An encyclopaedia is a large book with much interesting information about the world and the people who live and work in it. In an encyclopaedia, information is set out so that the learner can read it easily, helped by many pictures and drawings. There is so much to be learned about our world that information about it could fill many encyclopaedias.

Peter is reading about coal, in an encyclopaedia. He learns that millions of years ago, trees on the surface of the earth sank very, very slowly below the surface. Through millions of years these buried trees very slowly turned into coal. The wood became coal—something like black rock and quite hard.

Now men bring this coal up to the surface of the earth to use it in many different ways.

On one page is a picture of what part of a forest may have looked like millions of years ago. There is another picture showing how trees in the forest sank very slowly below the earth's surface.

The last drawing is of a coal mine. It shows how the coal is brought up to the surface for men to use.

Coal was first used to burn to keep people warm. Coal fires are still found in many houses. Coal is also used to make some of the gas and electricity needed today.

We learn that coal is also used in the making of tar, dyes, paint, nylon, drugs and plastics.

Tar is often used in making a road, a roof of a building or a ship. Most clothes, furnishings and fabrics have dyes in them. Nearly every building and car has been painted. Nylon is found in many clothes, furnishings, ropes and parachutes. Most doctors use drugs. New things made of plastic appear almost every day. Something of plastic can be found in nearly every house. Children's toys are often made of this, and many clothes.

These are only some of the things made from coal. It is very interesting to know that the trees of long ago, which were turned into coal deep under the earth, can now be used by man in so many valuable ways.

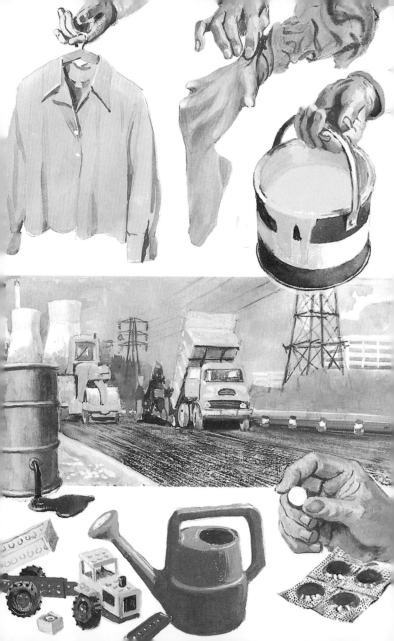

Jane borrows the encyclopaedia from Peter and turns the pages. She looks first at the pictures, and then reads what is printed by them. "It seems an easy and interesting way to learn," she says.

"Here is a dressing-table like ours," she says. "It is an oak dressing-table, made of wood from the oak tree. Barrels and boats and gates can be made from oak. It is a hard wood."

"Some of our furniture is made of walnut," says Peter. "That is another hard wood."

"Yes," answers his sister. "There is a picture of a walnut tree here, with furniture made of walnut. It shows other things which can be made from walnut wood."

"My cricket bat is made of willow," says Peter.

"Yes," says Jane, "cricket bats, some baskets, toys and fencing are made from willow. It is not as hard as oak or walnut."

Peter comes over to look at the book. "There is a picture of a pine tree," he says. "Doors, windows and boxes are often made from pine wood."

The children continue to look through the encyclopaedia. They read how some other kinds of soft wood are made into paper for newspapers, comics and books.

Oak   Walnut   Willow   Pine

The two children are so interested in the encyclopaedia that they go on reading and looking at the pictures.

They learn that trees from which paper is made are grown in Canada, Norway and Sweden. The trees are cut down and the logs floated down the rivers. The logs are made into large rafts, and men stand on these to make sure the logs keep moving. Sometimes they are on the log rafts for a long time. They take the logs to the mills, where they are cut up and made into pulp-boards to send to paper-mills in different parts of the world.

At the paper-mills the boards are made into pulp. China-clay and other things are added to the pulp and then it is poured into a very large paper-making machine. Pulp, looking something like milk, goes in at one end of the machine and paper comes out at the other.

These large rolls of paper are put on lorries and driven to printers for making into newspapers and books.

The children then turn over the pages to read what happens to the paper when it gets to the printer.

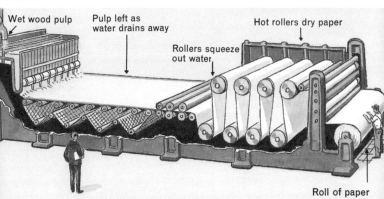

Wet wood pulp

Pulp left as water drains away

Rollers squeeze out water

Hot rollers dry paper

Roll of paper

MAKING A BOOK

The words for a book are set on a special machine called a photo-typesetter. This machine does its work as quickly as a man can type on a special keyboard that looks like a typewriter.

Then large sheets of paper are printed by huge machines which run at speeds as fast as 10,000 sheets an hour. The machines can print four or more colours at once, if coloured illustrations are included. When the sheets are printed they are collected by special fork-lift trucks and taken to a large warehouse, where they are stored.

When the printed sheets go into the binding room, they are cut to size by huge cutters called guillotines. These guillotines can cut as many as 500 sheets at a time. Then the sheets are folded at high speeds in special folding machines. Meanwhile, the covers of the book are being prepared.

Finally, the inside of the book is put into the covers automatically, and again at high speed, by more special machinery.

The books then go to another warehouse until they are needed in the shops.

Photo-typesetting

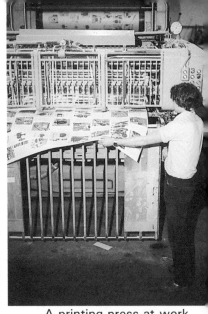

A printing press at work

A warehouse

A guillotine cuts the sheets

Some more help with sounds*

Three sounds of ed

We have learned that after the consonants k, ck, p, sh and ss the suffix **ed** is generally sounded like **t**. *Examples*—cooked, kicked, hoped, pushed, dressed.

This is also true after the consonants c, f, ph, x and ch. *Examples*—raced, sniffed, photographed, mixed, reached.

After d and t the suffix **ed** forms an additional syllable. *Examples we know*—crowded, counted, decided, fitted, floated, lasted, sounded, waited.

New words to learn—bolted, demanded, descended, enchanted, hated, hooted, invited, mounted, roasted, scolded, twisted.

In nearly all other words **ed** is pronounced d. *Examples we know*—answered, called, disappeared, entered, frightened, moved, owned, planned, pulled, remembered, turned, whispered, belonged.

New words to learn—aimed, amused, begged, dragged, ordered, showed, stayed, wandered, wondered.

*See also Books 4c to 10c.

Two sounds of ow

We have learned the sound of **OW** in
cow, how, now, flower.

But **OW** is pronounced as a long **O** in some
words. *Examples we know*—below, blow, flow,
know, low, row, show, slow, throw, tomorrow,
yellow, window.

New words to learn—arrow, crossbow, glow,
narrow, shadow, swallow, sorrow, snow.

Three sounds of o

We have learned the sounds of **O** as in
(1) orange, ostrich, otter, ox, dog, hot, log,
    not, pot, shop, stop, top.

(2) go, no, so.

(3) Now we find that **O** is pronounced as a short
u in—another, become, love, money, mother,
nothing, sometimes, somewhere, sons.

New words to learn—among, front, none, oven,
sponge, tongue, wonder.

The soft sound of c

We have learned one sound of **C** in the words car, cow, cat, cap, camp, call, cut, card, cane, cook, coat, candle, etc.

In some other words we know, the sound of **C** is soft. *Examples*—ice, nice, dice, mice, race, face, place, except, dancing, once, etc.

New words to learn. The **C** in each of them has a soft sound—cell, cider, city, fancy, lance, mercy, spice.

In the words council and scarce, the two **C**'s in each word have different sounds.

The soft sound of g

We have learned the sound of **g** as in girl, gun, gate, goose, go, get, game, goat, good, etc.

In some other words we know, the sound of **g** is soft. *Examples*—bridge, edge, giant, gipsy, large.

New words to learn, each of which has a soft **g** — change, cartridge, cottage, courage, dodge, fringe, general, gentle, hinge, huge, imagine, judge, lodge, magic, manage, oblige, porridge.

ar   er   or   our

In the following words **ar, er, or** and **our** are pronounced nearly alike.

ar	er	or	our
beggar	butcher	victor	colour
burglar	mother	author	valour
calendar	another	mirror	vigour
cellar	smaller	councillor	clamour
circular	shoulder	anchor	harbour
collar	pointer	error	vapour
dollar	danger	doctor	endeavour
jaguar	deserter	tailor	favour
sugar	monster	mayor	labour
pedlar	partner	horror	honour
pillar	outer	equator	humour
popular	corner	sailor	rumour
scholar	offer	governor	parlour
similar	stagger	emperor	neighbour
vinegar	either	terror	flavour

Learning by sounds

If children learn the sounds of letters and how to blend them with the other letter sounds (eg. c-a-t) they can tackle new words independently (eg. P-a-t).

In the initial stages it is best if these phonic words are already known to the learner.

However, not all English words can be learned in this way as the English language is not purely phonetic (eg. t-h-e).

In general a 'mixed' approach to reading is recommended. Some words are learned by blending the sounds of their letters and others by look-and-say, whole word or sentence methods.

This book provides the link with writing for the words in Readers 11a and 11b.